FIBER COOKING

Edited by
Carole Handslip

Contents

This edition first published 1979 by
Octopus Books Limited
59 Grosvenor Street, London W.1.

© 1979 Octopus Books Limited

ISBN 0 7064 1012 2

Produced and printed in Hong Kong by
Mandarin Publishers Limited
22a Westlands Road, Quarry Bay

Frontispiece: FRESH FRUIT AND VEGETABLES
(Photograph: Carmel Produce Information Bureau)

Weights and Measures

All measurements in this book are based on Imperial weights and measures, with American equivalents given in parenthesis.

Measurements in *weight* in the Imperial and American system are the same. Liquid measurements are different, and the following table shows the equivalents:

Liquid measurements
1 Imperial pint .... 20 fluid ounces
1 American pint .... 16 fluid ounces
1 American cup .... 8 fluid ounces

Level spoon measurements are used in all the recipes.

Spoon measurements
1 tablespoon (1T).. 15 ml
1 teaspoon .... 5 ml

INTRODUCTION

The use of natural foods in cooking has enjoyed a great revival in the last few years. By the terms wholefoods and natural foods, we mean foods grown in natural conditions, which are virtually unprocessed and contain no artificial colourings, flavourings or preservatives. These foods retain their natural flavour and are prepared with as little loss as possible of the nutrients they contain. Wholefoods are preferably eaten raw or very simply cooked to preserve the valuable vitamin and mineral content which is so important for a balanced and healthy diet.

Eating wholefoods does not mean avoiding meat or becoming a vegetarian. But care should be taken when buying meat or poultry; there are 'free range' meats available from some specialist natural food stores or country butchers but these can be expensive.

A wholefood diet will benefit all members of the family. Nutritionally whole grains are an ideal source of many of our basic dietary requirements (proteins, carbohydrates, oils, vitamins, minerals, and fibre). The grain starches are broken down during the process of digestion to form glucose, which provides a constant supply of energy to the body. White sugar, on the other hand, passes rapidly into the bloodstream giving a quick 'boost' to the system which soon disappears. The fibre in whole grains provides the intestine with essential roughage. Vegetables and fruit also contain fibre but this is slightly different from cereal fibre. It is an excellent idea to include a combination of the two sources in the diet.

A few years ago cooking with natural food was difficult to do as there were few shops which supplied unprocessed foods. Today, natural foods are widely available throughout the country, either by mail order, through local stores, or from your own garden, and so interest in this type of cookery has increased dramatically. Natural foods presently available include wholewheat bread and flour products; whole grains, pure honey, organically grown fruit and vegetables, dried fruits, nuts and natural yogurt. Dried beans and peas have also increased in popularity. They are as rich in protein as meat and are an excellent source of the B vitamins and iron. Their high food value makes them invaluable to the vegetarian diet.

This book contains a whole range of recipes from appetizers and salads through to delicious cakes, cookies and breads. The aim is to provide a choice of dishes with the emphasis on flavour, texture and food value.

MUSHROOM BREAD *(page 82)*, MUSHROOM TERRINE *(page 10)*
(Photograph: Mushroom Growers' Association)

APPETIZERS AND SALADS

Mushroom Terrine

12 oz. (3 cups) mushrooms,
  chopped
6 oz. (¾ cup) minced (ground)
  cooked ham
12 oz. (1½ cups) minced (ground)
  pork
3 oz. (½ cup) onion, minced
  (ground)
1½ oz. (¾ cup) fresh wholemeal
  (wholewheat) breadcrumbs

2 tomatoes, skinned and chopped
1 tablespoon chopped fresh parsley
1 teaspoon chopped fresh thyme
1 tablespoon soy sauce
1 large egg
sea salt
freshly ground black pepper

Place all the ingredients in a bowl and mix together thoroughly.
Turn into an earthenware terrine, cover with foil, and bake in a
moderately hot oven, 375°F, Gas Mark 5 for 1-1½ hours. Serve with
crusty wholemeal (wholewheat) bread.
Serves 8

Nut-stuffed Mushrooms

4 large mushrooms
1 tablespoon oil
2 tablespoons chopped pine nuts
1 clove garlic, crushed
2 tablespoons fresh wholemeal
  (wholewheat) breadcrumbs
2 teaspoons chopped fresh parsley

2 teaspoons chopped fresh chives
2 tablespoons cream
sea salt
freshly ground black pepper
2 oz. (½ cup) Cheddar cheese,
  grated

Remove the stalks from the mushrooms and chop them finely. Heat
the oil in a pan and fry the mushroom stalks, pine nuts and garlic for
a few minutes, then stir in the breadcrumbs, herbs, cream and
seasoning and mix well.

Place the mushroom caps on a greased baking sheet, fill with the
stuffing and sprinkle with the cheese. Bake in a moderate oven,
350°F, Gas Mark 4 for 20-30 minutes.
Serves 4

Bulgur Wheat Salad

6 oz. (1 cup) bulgur wheat
6 spring onions (scallions), chopped
4 tablespoons chopped fresh parsley
4 tablespoons chopped fresh mint
2 tablespoons soy sauce
3 tablespoons olive oil

1 tablespoon lemon juice
sea salt
freshly ground black pepper
Garnish:
2 tomatoes, sliced
black olives

Soak the bulgur wheat for 30 minutes, drain and dry well on kitchen
paper. Add the spring onions (scallions), parsley, mint, soy sauce,
olive oil, lemon juice and seasoning and mix thoroughly. Garnish
with tomato slices and black olives.
Serves 6

Mixed Bean Salad

4 oz. (½ cup) haricot (navy) beans, soaked overnight and drained

4 oz. (⅓ cup) red kidney beans, soaked overnight and drained

4 oz. (⅔ cup) butter beans, soaked overnight and drained

4 spring onions (scallions), finely chopped

1 red pepper, seeded and finely chopped

chopped fresh parsley to garnish

Dressing:

6 tablespoons olive oil

2 tablespoons cider vinegar

1 clove garlic, crushed

pinch of dry English mustard

sea salt

freshly ground black pepper

Cook the beans separately for 1-1½ hours, as some will take longer to soften than others. Add salt towards the end of cooking. When cooked, drain the beans, mix together and add the onions and pepper.

To make the dressing, mix the oil, vinegar, garlic, mustard and seasoning in a screw-top jar and shake well. Pour the dressing over the bean salad, mix lightly and leave to stand for 1 hour. Adjust seasoning and serve sprinkled with parsley.

Serves 6

Wheat and Pepper Salad

8 oz. (1¾ cups) wheat, soaked overnight and drained

1 red pepper, seeded and chopped

2 oz. (⅓ cup) raisins, chopped

2 oz. (½ cup) blanched almonds, toasted

2 tablespoons chopped fresh parsley

Dressing:

4 tablespoons olive oil

2 tablespoons soy sauce

1 tablespoon lemon juice

sea salt

freshly ground black pepper

Cover the wheat with lightly salted cold water, bring to the boil and simmer for 1-1½ hours, then drain and mix with the pepper, raisins, almonds and parsley.

To make the dressing, mix the oil, soy sauce, lemon juice and seasoning in a screw-top jar and shake well. Pour over the salad and toss until thoroughly coated.

Serves 4-6

MIXED BEAN SALAD
(Photograph: Paul Williams)

Red Bean and Olive Salad

6 oz. (⅔ cup) red kidney beans,
  soaked overnight and drained
sea salt
4 sticks celery, chopped
4 tomatoes, skinned and chopped
12 black olives, stoned (pitted) and
  halved

1 teaspoon chopped fresh chives
1 teaspoon chopped fresh mint
Dressing:
4 tablespoons olive oil
1 tablespoon cider vinegar
freshly ground black pepper

Cover the beans with water, bring to the boil and simmer for 1½
hours, adding salt towards the end of cooking. Drain and cool, then
mix with the celery, tomatoes, olives, chives and mint.

Mix the oil, vinegar and seasoning in a screw-top jar and shake
well. Pour over the salad and toss until thoroughly coated.
Serves 4

Bean Shoot and Mushroom Salad

8 oz. (4 cups) bean shoots, washed
  and drained
12 oz. (3 cups) button mushrooms,
  washed and quartered
1 red pepper, seeded and diced
chopped fresh parsley to garnish

Dressing:
4 tablespoons olive oil
1 tablespoon cider vinegar
1 clove garlic, crushed
1 teaspoon soy sauce
sea salt
freshly ground black pepper

Place the vegetables in a salad bowl.

To make the dressing, mix the oil, vinegar, garlic, soy sauce and
seasoning in a screw-top jar and shake well. Pour over the salad
ingredients and toss until well coated.

Serve sprinkled with the parsley.
Serves 4

Winter Salad

2 oz. (½ cup) wholemeal
  (wholewheat) cut macaroni
2 carrots, cut into matchsticks
¼ celeriac or 2 sticks celery, cut
  into matchsticks
½ small white cabbage, finely
  shredded
2 dessert apples, cored and finely
  sliced
2 tablespoons raisins
2 tablespoons walnuts, coarsely
  chopped
chopped fresh parsley to garnish

Dressing:
¼ pint (⅔ cup) natural
  (unflavored) yogurt
1 tablespoon vinegar
1 tablespoon clear honey
sea salt
freshly ground black pepper

Cook the macaroni in boiling salted water for 20 minutes, rinse in cold water, drain well and add to the vegetables, fruit and nuts.

Make the dressing by mixing the yogurt, vinegar, honey and seasoning. Pour over the salad, mix well and serve sprinkled with the parsley.

Serves 4-6

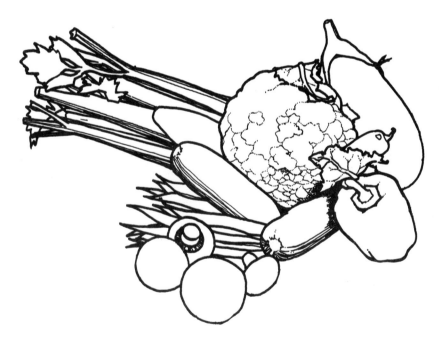

Lentil Salad

6 oz. (¾ cup) green lentils
6 tablespoons French dressing
1 clove garlic, crushed
sea salt

4 spring onions (scallions), chopped
4 tomatoes, skinned and chopped
2 sticks celery, chopped
freshly ground black pepper

Soak the lentils for 1 hour, then cook in slightly salted water for 25-30 minutes until tender. Drain well and mix with the French dressing, garlic, and salt while still warm. Add the remaining ingredients and mix thoroughly.
Serves 4

Red Cabbage Salad

2 dessert apples, peeled, cored and
  thinly sliced
1 lb. (6 cups) red cabbage, finely
  shredded
1 bunch watercress, washed and
  sprigged
2 tablespoons sultanas (seedless
  white raisins)
chopped fresh parsley to garnish

Dressing:
4 tablespoons olive oil
1 tablespoon cider vinegar
1 clove garlic, crushed
½ teaspoon French mustard
sea salt
freshly ground black pepper

To prepare the dressing, mix the oil, vinegar, garlic, mustard and seasoning in a screw-top jar and shake well.

Pour this dressing over the apples in a bowl and toss to coat them completely. Mix in the cabbage, watercress and sultanas (seedless white raisins). Toss well and serve sprinkled with the parsley.
Serves 4

LENTIL SALAD
(Photograph: Paul Williams)

Brown Rice Salad

8 oz. (1 cup + 2T) brown rice, washed
3 spring onions (scallions), finely chopped
2 oz. (⅓ cup) currants
2 oz. (½ cup) peanuts, chopped
1 small red pepper, seeded and chopped
1 small green pepper, seeded and chopped
sea salt
freshly ground black pepper
4 tablespoons French dressing

Cook the rice in plenty of boiling, salted water for 1 hour, or until tender. Drain and rinse under cold water to separate the grains. Drain again thoroughly and transfer to a bowl.

Stir in the spring onions (scallions), currants, peanuts, peppers and seasoning. Pour the French dressing over the salad and mix thoroughly.

Serves 4-6

Walnut and Avocado Salad

2 ripe avocados
a little lemon juice
1 green pepper, seeded and chopped
2 oz. (½ cup) walnuts, chopped

Dressing:
3 tablespoons oil
1 tablespoon cider vinegar
1 clove garlic, crushed
pinch of dry English mustard
sea salt
freshly ground black pepper

Cut the avocados in half and remove the stones (pits). Scrape the flesh gently into a bowl, without damaging the skins. Mash the flesh with the lemon juice and mix in the pepper and walnuts.

Put the oil, vinegar, garlic, mustard, salt and pepper into a screw-top jar and shake thoroughly. Add to the avocado mixture and mix well. Spoon into the avocado skins.

Serve with thin slices of buttered wholewheat bread.

Serves 4

Aduki Bean and Mushroom Salad

2 oz. (¼ cup) green aduki beans,
  soaked overnight and drained
sea salt
12 oz. (3 cups) button mushrooms
1 tablespoon chopped fresh parsley
1 teaspoon chopped fresh thyme

Dressing:
3 tablespoons olive oil
1 tablespoon cider vinegar
sea salt
freshly ground black pepper
pinch of dry English mustard
1 clove garlic, crushed

Cover the beans with cold water, bring to the boil then simmer gently for 1 hour, adding salt towards the end of cooking. Drain and allow to cool.

Wash the mushrooms, trim the stalks level with the caps, cut into quarters and place in a bowl with the parsley, thyme and cooled beans.

Place the oil, vinegar, salt, pepper, mustard and garlic in a screw-top jar and shake well. Pour over the salad and leave to stand in the refrigerator for at least 1 hour before serving.
Serves 4-6

Date and Apple Salad

4 oz. (²⁄₃ cup) fresh dates, skinned
 and stoned (pitted)
2 red-skinned dessert apples, cored
 and diced
3 sticks celery, finely sliced
2 oz. (½ cup) walnuts, chopped
8 Chinese leaves, shredded

Dressing:
¼ pint (²⁄₃ cup) natural
 (unflavored) yogurt
1 tablespoon clear honey
juice of ½ lemon
sea salt
freshly ground black pepper

Prepare the dressing by mixing the yogurt, honey, lemon juice and
seasoning.

Cut the dates into quarters and add to the dressing, together with
the apples, celery and walnuts. Spoon the salad onto a bed of Chinese
leaves and serve.
Serves 4

Celery, Apple and Walnut Salad

3 red-skinned dessert apples, cored
 and finely sliced
1 head of celery, finely sliced
2 oz. (½ cup) walnuts, coarsely
 chopped
chopped fresh parsley to garnish

Dressing:
3 tablespoons olive oil
1 tablespoon cider vinegar
pinch of dry English mustard
sea salt
freshly ground black pepper

Put the apples and celery into a bowl with the chopped nuts.

To make the dressing, mix the oil, vinegar, mustard and seasoning
in a screw-top jar and shake well. Pour the dressing over the apple
and celery mixture and toss well.

Spoon into a serving dish and sprinkle with chopped parsley.
Serves 4

BEAN AND BACON SOUP *(page 22)*
(Photograph: Paul Williams)

SOUPS

Bean and Bacon Soup

2 tablespoons oil
1 onion, chopped
1 clove garlic, crushed
2½ pints (6¼ cups) stock
8 oz. (1¼ cups) butter beans,
  soaked overnight and drained
1 lb. piece of bacon

1 bay leaf
sprig of fresh thyme
freshly ground black pepper
2 tablespoons chopped fresh parsley
10 black olives, halved and stoned
  (pitted)

Heat the oil in a large saucepan and fry the onion and garlic for a few minutes, until softened, then add the stock, beans, bacon, herbs and pepper. Bring to the boil, reduce the heat and simmer the soup for 1½ hours until the beans are tender.

Remove the herbs and the bacon and cut the bacon into cubes. Purée half the beans in a blender with some of the liquid, or press through a sieve (strainer).

Return to the saucepan with the bacon cubes, parsley and olives. Reheat, adjust the seasoning to taste and serve.
Serves 6–8

Lentil and Vegetable Soup

2 tablespoons oil
1 onion, peeled and chopped
1 clove garlic, crushed
2 sticks celery, chopped
1 carrot, peeled and chopped

2 tomatoes, peeled and chopped
4 oz. (½ cup) red lentils
sea salt
freshly ground black pepper
1¾ pints (4¼ cups) stock

Heat the oil and fry the onion and garlic until soft. Add the remaining ingredients and simmer for 40 minutes until the lentils and vegetables are tender. Adjust the seasoning to taste, and serve with crusty wholemeal (wholewheat) bread.
Serves 6

Spinach and Cheese Soup

1 lb. spinach
2 tablespoons oil
1 onion, finely chopped
1 tablespoon wholemeal
  (wholewheat) flour
1¼ pints (3 cups) stock
sea salt

freshly ground black pepper
pinch of grated nutmeg
3 oz. (¾ cup) Cheddar cheese,
  grated
¼ pint (⅔ cup) single (light)
  cream

Cook the spinach in boiling, salted water for 5 minutes, drain and chop roughly.

Heat the oil in a saucepan and cook the onion gently for 5 minutes. Mix in the flour and then gradually stir in the stock with the salt, pepper and nutmeg to taste. Bring to the boil, add the spinach, cover and simmer for 15 minutes, stirring occasionally.

Purée the soup in a blender, then return to the rinsed-out saucepan and add the cheese and cream. Reheat but do not allow to boil. Adjust the seasoning to taste. If liked, serve with croûtons.
Serves 4

Spicy Lentil Soup

2 tablespoons oil
2 onions, chopped
2 cloves garlic, crushed
8 oz. (1 cup) red lentils
1 3/4 pints (4 1/4 cups) water
1 bay leaf
1/2 teaspoon ground ginger

1/2 teaspoon ground turmeric
2 teaspoons curry powder
sea salt
freshly ground black pepper
lemon juice
chopped fresh parsley to garnish

Heat the oil in a pan and cook the onions and garlic until soft but not
coloured. Add the lentils, water, bay leaf, ginger, turmeric, curry
powder and seasoning. Bring to the boil and simmer gently for 45
minutes, stirring occasionally. Sharpen with lemon juice to taste,
adjust the seasoning and serve sprinkled with chopped parsley.
Serves 6

Jerusalem Artichoke Soup

1 tablespoon oil
1 large onion, peeled and sliced
1 1/2 lb. Jerusalem artichokes, peeled
 and roughly chopped
1 pint (2 1/2 cups) chicken stock
sea salt

freshly ground black pepper
pinch of grated nutmeg
squeeze of lemon juice
1/4 pint (2/3 cup) single (light)
 cream
chopped fresh parsley to garnish

Heat the oil in a pan and cook the onion until transparent, then add
the artichokes and cook for a further 5 minutes. Pour the stock into
the pan, cover and simmer for about 30 minutes.

   Allow to cool, then purée to a cream in a blender or pass through a
sieve (strainer). Return to the rinsed-out pan, add seasoning to taste,
nutmeg, a squeeze of lemon juice and the cream. Reheat and serve
garnished with chopped parsley.
Serves 4

SPICY LENTIL SOUP
(Photograph: Paul Williams)

Leek and Potato Soup

2 tablespoons oil
1 lb. (4½ cups) leeks, cleaned and sliced
1 small onion, peeled and sliced
2 medium potatoes, peeled and sliced

1 clove garlic, crushed
1 pint (2½ cups) chicken stock
sea salt
freshly ground black pepper
chopped fresh chives to garnish

Heat the oil in a large saucepan and fry the vegetables and garlic for about 5 minutes until soft. Add the stock and seasoning and bring to the boil. Reduce the heat and simmer, covered, for 30 minutes, until the potatoes are well cooked.

Sieve (strain) the soup, or purée in a blender. Return to the rinsed-out pan, reheat and adjust the seasoning to taste. Serve garnished with chopped chives.
Serves 4

Minestra

2 tablespoons oil
2 onions, chopped
2 carrots, chopped
3 sticks celery, chopped
2 cloves garlic, crushed
3 oz. (½ cup) butter beans, soaked overnight and drained
1 bouquet garni
2½ pints (6¼ cups) stock

1 leek, cleaned and sliced
2 tablespoons tomato purée
2 tomatoes, skinned and chopped
1 oz. (¼ cup) French (green) beans, cut into 1 inch lengths
sea salt
freshly ground black pepper
chopped fresh parsley to garnish

Heat the oil in a pan and fry the onions, carrots, celery and garlic for a few minutes, then add the butter beans, bouquet garni and stock. Bring slowly to the boil, cover and simmer for about 1 hour.

Add the leek, tomato purée, tomatoes, French (green) beans and seasoning and simmer for a further 30–40 minutes. Adjust the seasoning and sprinkle with the parsley. If liked, serve with grated cheese.
Serves 8

Split Pea and Ham Soup

2 tablespoons oil
1 large onion, sliced
1 large carrot, sliced
1 stick celery, sliced
4 oz. (½ cup) split peas, soaked
  overnight and drained

4 oz. piece of ham or bacon
2 pints (5 cups) stock
¼ pint (⅔ cup) double (heavy)
  cream
sea salt
freshly ground black pepper

Heat the oil in a 4 pint (10 cup) saucepan. Add the onion, carrot and celery, and cook gently for 5 minutes, then stir in the split peas, ham and stock. Bring slowly to the boil, cover, and simmer for 2½ hours.

Remove the ham and cut into cubes. Purée the vegetables in a blender, or rub through a sieve (strainer). Return the purée to the rinsed-out pan with the ham and stock.

Just before serving, stir in the fresh cream, reheat and add seasoning to taste.
Serves 4

Scotch Broth

1 lb. middle neck of lamb
2 pints (5 cups) water
2 oz. (¼ cup) pearl barley
sea salt
freshly ground black pepper
2 onions, finely chopped

4 carrots, finely chopped
2 medium turnips, finely chopped
2 leeks, cleaned and thinly sliced
1 oz. (½ cup) bran
chopped fresh parsley to garnish

Place the meat in a saucepan with the water, bring to the boil and skim. Add the barley and seasoning, cover and cook gently for 30 minutes, then add the vegetables and bran. Continue cooking for a further 1½ hours.

Lift out the lamb, remove the meat from the bone and cut into small pieces. Return the meat to the pan, adjust the seasoning and add more liquid if required. Serve sprinkled with the parsley.
Serves 4

Haricot Bean (Navy Bean) Soup

8 oz. (1 cup) haricot (navy) beans,
  soaked overnight and drained
1½ pints (3¾ cups) water
sea salt
1 tablespoon olive oil

1 medium onion, sliced
1 medium potato, sliced
1 clove garlic, crushed
freshly ground black pepper
chopped fresh parsley to garnish

Cover the beans with the water and cook for 1½–2 hours, until they are soft, adding salt towards the end of cooking. Heat the oil in a large pan and fry the onion, potato and garlic for 5 minutes.

Purée half the beans in a blender with half the water in which they were cooked, then add this purée, with the remainder of the beans, to the onion and potato mixture and bring to the boil. Season to taste, and cook for a further 20 minutes.

Serve sprinkled with the chopped parsley.
Serves 4-6

Cucumber Soup

2 large cucumbers, peeled and
  chopped
1 ½ pints (3 ¾ cups) chicken stock
1 small onion

¼ pint (⅔ cup) soured cream
sea salt
freshly ground black pepper
chopped fresh mint to garnish

Put the cucumber, stock and onion into a saucepan, bring to the boil, cover and simmer for 10 minutes or until the cucumber is tender.

Pass the soup through a sieve (strainer) or purée in a blender. Blend a little of the soup with the soured cream, then add this to the remainder of the soup, with the seasoning.

Serve chilled and sprinkled with chopped mint.
Serves 4

Iced Avocado Soup

2 avocados
¾ pint (2 cups) chicken stock
½ teaspoon grated onion
1 teaspoon lemon juice
½ teaspoon Worcestershire sauce
½ pint (1 ¼ cups) natural
  (unflavored) yogurt

¼ pint (⅔ cup) single (light)
  cream
sea salt
freshly ground black pepper
chopped fresh chives to garnish

Peel the avocados, remove the stones (pits) and place in a blender with the stock and the remaining ingredients. Blend for 1 minute, adjust the seasoning and dilute with more stock if the mixture is too thick.

Place in the refrigerator for 30 minutes before serving. Serve ice cold and sprinkled with chives.
Serves 4-6

VEGETABLES

Red Cabbage with Hazelnuts

1 ½ lb. (9 cups) red cabbage,
  shredded
2 tablespoons oil
1 onion, sliced
2 oz. (⅓ cup) hazelnuts, chopped
4 dessert apples, quartered, cored
  and finely sliced

2 tablespoons clear honey
4 tablespoons cider vinegar
2 tablespoons lemon juice
¼ pint (⅔ cup) stock
sea salt
freshly ground black pepper

Blanch the cabbage in boiling water for 3 minutes and drain. Heat
the oil in a large pan, add the onion and hazelnuts and cook gently
for 5 minutes. Stir in the cabbage, apples and all the remaining
ingredients.

Cover and cook over a low heat for 20 minutes, stirring
occasionally. Adjust the seasoning before serving.
Serves 4

Mushroom-stuffed Tomatoes

4 large tomatoes, washed
2 tablespoons oil
4 oz. (1 cup) button mushrooms,
 finely chopped
2 shallots, finely chopped
2 tablespoons fresh wholemeal
 (wholewheat) breadcrumbs

1 oz. (¼ cup) hazelnuts, ground
1 teaspoon chopped fresh thyme
1 teaspoon chopped fresh parsley
sea salt
freshly ground black pepper
1 tablespoon cheese, finely grated

Slice the top off each tomato and carefully scoop out the seeds.

Heat the oil in a pan and cook the mushrooms and shallots for a few minutes, then stir in the breadcrumbs, nuts, herbs, seasoning and cheese. Fill the tomatoes with this mixture and replace the tops.

Cook in a moderate oven, 350°F, Gas Mark 4 for about 15 minutes.
Serves 4

Lentil and Spinach Croquettes

4 oz. (½ cup) red lentils
1 lb. spinach
6 oz. (3 cups) fresh wholemeal
 (wholewheat) breadcrumbs
1 egg
½ teaspoon grated nutmeg

sea salt
freshly ground black pepper
oil for shallow frying
Coating:
beaten egg
breadcrumbs

Soak the lentils for 30 minutes, then drain. Add enough fresh water to cover and simmer for 20 minutes until the water is absorbed and the lentils are quite dry.

Cook the spinach in lightly salted water for 5–10 minutes, drain well and chop finely.

Mix the lentils, spinach, breadcrumbs, egg, nutmeg and seasoning and form into 12 croquettes. Coat in beaten egg and breadcrumbs and fry in shallow oil until golden.
Serves 4

MUSHROOM-STUFFED TOMATO
(Photograph: Paul Williams)

Mushrooms with Coriander

3 tablespoons oil
8 oz. (1 cup) streaky (fatty) bacon,
  chopped
1 onion, chopped
1 lb. (4 cups) button mushrooms,
  quartered
1 tablespoon wholemeal
  (wholewheat) flour

¼ pint (⅔ cup) stock
1 teaspoon ground coriander
sea salt
freshly ground black pepper
¼ pint (⅔ cup) single (light)
  cream
chopped fresh parsley to garnish

Heat the oil in a pan, add the bacon and onion and cook for 5 minutes. Add the mushrooms and continue cooking gently for a further 10 minutes, stirring occasionally.

Sprinkle in the flour and mix well, then gradually add the stock and bring to the boil, stirring constantly. Add the coriander, seasoning and cream and simmer for a few minutes to heat through. Serve garnished with the parsley.
Serves 4

Ratatouille

4 tablespoons olive oil
2 large onions, sliced
1 red pepper, seeded and sliced
1 green pepper, seeded and sliced
2 medium aubergines (eggplant),
  sliced

2 cloves garlic, crushed
8 oz. (1½ cups) courgettes
  (zucchini), sliced
6 large tomatoes, skinned and sliced
sea salt
freshly ground black pepper

Heat the oil in a large pan and cook the onion gently for 5 minutes or until soft. Add the peppers, aubergines (eggplant) and garlic and cook for a further 10 minutes, stirring occasionally.

Add the courgettes (zucchini), tomatoes and seasoning, cover the pan and simmer very gently for 30 minutes. Remove the lid and continue cooking for 10 minutes.
Serves 4

Mixed Vegetable Pickle

12 oz. (1¼ cups) red kidney
  beans, soaked overnight and
  drained
4 red peppers, seeded and cut into
  2 inch pieces
1 medium cauliflower, broken into
  florets
1 lb. (4 cups) French (green) beans,
  cut into 2 inch lengths

sea salt
1 × 14 oz. can sweetcorn (kernel
  corn), drained
2 pints (5 cups) cider vinegar
6 oz. (1 cup) molasses sugar
3 tablespoons mustard seed
5 tablespoons dry mustard
1 teaspoon ground turmeric

Place the kidney beans in a pan, cover with water, bring to the boil
and simmer for 1-1½ hours until just tender, then drain.

Blanch the peppers, cauliflower and French (green) beans in
boiling salted water for 5 minutes, drain and mix with the kidney
beans and corn.

Heat the vinegar in a pan with the sugar, mustard seed, dry
mustard and turmeric, until the sugar has dissolved. Add the
vegetables and simmer gently for 5 minutes. Allow to cool slightly,
then ladle the pickle into warmed preserving jars. Seal, label and
store in a cool dry place.
Makes 3½ lb.

Dhal

1 tablespoon oil
1 onion, finely chopped
1 clove garlic, crushed
½ teaspoon ground turmeric
1 teaspoon ground coriander
1 teaspoon curry powder

6 oz. (¾ cup) red lentils, soaked
  for 30 minutes and drained
1 pint (2½ cups) stock
sea salt
freshly ground black pepper

Heat the oil in a pan and fry the onion until soft. Stir in the garlic,
turmeric, coriander and curry powder and cook for a further 2
minutes over a low heat.

Add the lentils, stock and seasoning, cover and cook gently for
50-60 minutes until the lentils are quite soft.

Dhal should be the consistency of a very thick pea soup. Adjust
the seasoning and serve with a curry.
Serves 6

Courgettes (Zucchini) with Corn

8 courgettes (zucchini)
2 tablespoons oil
1 onion, chopped
1 × 7 oz. can sweetcorn (kernel
 corn), drained

4 oz. (1 cup) Cheddar cheese,
 grated
2 oz. (½ cup) walnuts, chopped
sea salt
freshly ground black pepper

Cut the courgettes (zucchini) in half lengthwise, scoop out the flesh and chop finely. Blanch the shells in boiling water for 2 minutes and drain well.

Heat the oil in a pan and fry the onion and courgette (zucchini) flesh for 5 minutes, until softened, then add the remaining ingredients and mix well.

Arrange the courgette (zucchini) shells in a shallow ovenproof casserole, fill with the mixture, cover and bake in a moderately hot oven, 375°F, Gas Mark 5 for 40 minutes.
Serves 6–8

Spiced Cauliflower

2 tablespoons oil
2 teaspoons ground coriander
1 teaspoon ground turmeric
1 cauliflower, divided into florets
2 carrots, thinly sliced
1 large onion, sliced

4 fl. oz. (½ cup) stock
¼ pint (⅔ cup) natural
 (unflavored) yogurt
sea salt
freshly ground black pepper

Heat the oil in a pan, add the spices and fry gently for 1 minute. Add the vegetables to the pan and cook gently for a further 5 minutes, stirring occasionally.

Add the stock, yogurt and seasoning, stir well, cover and simmer for 10 minutes, or until the vegetables are just tender.
Serves 4

COURGETTES (ZUCCHINI) WITH CORN
(Photograph: Paul Williams)

HIGH PROTEIN VEGETABLE DISHES

Hungarian Spinach Pancakes

Batter:
½ pint (1¼ cups) milk and water, mixed
1 egg
4 oz. (1 cup) wholemeal (wholewheat) flour
1 teaspoon sea salt
1 tablespoon oil

Filling:
1 lb. fresh spinach
1 tablespoon oil
1 onion, chopped
1 teaspoon paprika pepper
2 teaspoons tomato purée
4 tomatoes, skinned and chopped
sea salt
freshly ground black pepper
2 oz. (½ cup) Cheddar cheese, grated, to finish

Place the milk and water, egg, flour, salt and oil in a blender and blend for 2 minutes. Pour into a jug (pitcher) and leave to stand for 30 minutes.

Cook the spinach in boiling, salted water, drain well and chop finely. Heat the oil in a pan and fry the onion until soft, then add the paprika and fry for a further 1 minute. Stir in the tomato purée, tomatoes and spinach, season well and mix thoroughly.

Using the prepared batter, fry 4 or 5 pancakes (crêpes). Place one on a heatproof plate, spread with some of the filling and cover with another pancake (crêpe). Continue layering in this way, finishing with a pancake (crêpe). Sprinkle with the cheese and bake in a moderately hot oven, 375°F, Gas Mark 5 for 30 minutes.
Serves 4

Split Pea and Vegetable Casserole

12 oz. (1½ cups) split peas
3 oz. (6 T) barley
2 pints (5 cups) stock
3 tablespoons olive oil
3 sticks celery, chopped
2 onions, sliced

2 carrots, sliced
2 potatoes, sliced
1 clove garlic, crushed
4 tomatoes, skinned and chopped
sea salt
freshly ground black pepper

Put the split peas and barley into a pan with the stock, bring to the boil and simmer for 1 hour.

Heat the oil in a flameproof casserole and add the celery, onions, carrots, potatoes and garlic. Fry for 5 minutes. Add the tomatoes and seasoning, then pour over the stock with the peas and barley.

Transfer to a moderate oven, 350°F, Gas Mark 4 and cook for 1 hour.

Serves 4

Brazil Nut Bake

2 tablespoons fine, dry, wholemeal
  (wholewheat) breadcrumbs
8 oz. (1⅓ cups) Brazil nuts,
  ground
5 oz. (2½ cups) fresh wholemeal
  (wholewheat) breadcrumbs
6 tomatoes, skinned and chopped
2 tablespoons soya flour

2 tablespoons rolled oats
6 tablespoons tomato juice
1 egg
2 teaspoons dried basil
2 teaspoons chopped fresh parsley
sea salt
freshly ground black pepper

Grease a medium ring mould and coat with the fine, dry
breadcrumbs. Place all the remaining ingredients in a bowl and mix
together thoroughly. Spoon the mixture into the mould and press
down well.

   Bake in a moderately hot oven, 375°F, Gas Mark 5, for 50 minutes.
Cool slightly and loosen around the edge of the mould with a knife.
Turn out onto a serving dish and fill the centre with broccoli, or any
other colourful cooked vegetable.
Serves 4

GREEN AND RED PEPPER QUICHE
(Photograph: Carmel Produce Information Bureau)

Fruit and Vegetable Curry

4 tablespoons oil
2 onions, sliced
2 cloves garlic, crushed
2 teaspoons ground coriander
2 teaspoons curry powder
1 teaspoon turmeric
1 teaspoon ground cumin
1 inch piece root ginger, peeled and
  chopped
½ pint (1¼ cups) stock
4 carrots, peeled and diced
4 potatoes, peeled and diced

1 small cauliflower, broken into
  florets
1 × 14 oz. can tomatoes
4 oz. (½ cup) dried apricots,
  soaked overnight and chopped
sea salt
3 oz. (¾ cup) blanched almonds,
  toasted
2 bananas, sliced
¼ pint (⅔ cup) natural
  (unflavored) yogurt

Heat the oil in a large pan and fry the onions until soft. Add the
garlic and the spices and cook for a further 1 minute.

Pour in the stock, then add the vegetables, apricots and salt. Bring
to the boil, cover and simmer for 40 minutes. Gently stir in the
almonds, bananas and the yogurt. Serve with brown rice.
Serves 4-6

Butterbean Curry

8 oz. (1¼ cups) butter beans,
  soaked overnight and drained
3 tablespoons oil
1 onion, chopped
2 teaspoons ground coriander
1 teaspoon curry powder
½ teaspoon ground turmeric
1 tablespoon wholemeal
  (wholewheat) flour

1 clove garlic, crushed
1 pint (2½ cups) stock
1 tablespoon tomato purée
4 tomatoes, skinned and chopped
sea salt
freshly ground black pepper

Cover the beans with water and cook for 1 hour until just tender,
adding salt towards the end of cooking.

Heat the oil in a pan and fry the onion until soft. Add the spices,
flour and garlic and cook for 1 minute. Pour in the stock, add the
tomato purée, tomatoes, drained beans and seasoning and simmer for
30 minutes.

Adjust the seasoning and serve with brown rice.
Serves 4

Potato and Tomato Pie

1 oz. (2 T) butter
1 oz. (¼ cup) wholemeal
  (wholewheat) flour
½ pint (1¼ cups) milk
4 oz. (1 cup) cheese, grated
1 lb. potatoes

2 onions, sliced
1 lb. tomatoes, skinned and sliced
sea salt
freshly ground black pepper
pinch of dried basil

Melt the butter in a pan, stir in the flour and gradually add the milk.
Bring to the boil, stirring continuously, and cook the sauce for 2-3
minutes. Add 2 oz. (½ cup) of the cheese and stir until melted.

Cook the potatoes in boiling, salted water, then slice thinly. Grease
a shallow, ovenproof dish and arrange the potatoes in layers with the
onions, tomatoes and cheese sauce, seasoning with salt, pepper and
basil between each layer. Finish with a layer of potato, sprinkle with
the remaining 2 oz. (½ cup) of cheese, and bake in a moderate oven,
350°F, Gas Mark 4 for 45 minutes.
Serves 4

Lentil Stew

2 tablespoons oil
1 carrot, diced
2 leeks, thinly sliced
1 onion, diced
2 sticks celery, thinly sliced
1 × 14 oz. can tomatoes

¼ pint (⅔ cup) stock
sea salt
freshly ground black pepper
1 teaspoon chopped fresh parsley
8 oz. (1 cup) red lentils

Heat the oil in a saucepan and fry the carrot, leeks, onion and celery until soft. Add the tomatoes, stock, seasoning, parsley and lentils and simmer gently for 1-1½ hours, stirring occasionally.

Serve with a green salad.

Serves 4

Mushroom and Nut Pilaff

4 tablespoons olive oil
8 oz. (1 cup + 2T) brown rice
1 onion, sliced
1 clove garlic, crushed
2 sticks celery, chopped
1 red pepper, seeded and chopped

1 green pepper, seeded and chopped
4 oz. (1 cup) cashew nuts, chopped
6 oz. (1½ cups) button
  mushrooms, quartered
sea salt
freshly ground black pepper

Heat 2 tablespoons of the oil in a large pan and fry the rice for 2-3 minutes. Cover with boiling water and cook for 45 minutes, then drain well.

Heat the remaining oil in a large pan and fry the onion until transparent. Add the garlic, celery, peppers, nuts and mushrooms and cook together for 5-7 minutes. Add the cooked rice and seasoning and simmer gently, stirring occasionally, until heated through. Serve with a green salad.

Serves 4

Stuffed Peppers

4 peppers, red or green
3 tablespoons oil
1 onion, chopped
1 clove garlic, crushed
8 oz. (1⅓ cups) cooked brown rice
2 tablespoons pineapple pieces

½ teaspoon dried oregano
1 teaspoon miso
sea salt
freshly ground black pepper
2 oz. (1 cup) fresh wholemeal
  (wholewheat) breadcrumbs

Cut the tops off the peppers, reserve these, then scoop out the pith and seeds. Blanch the peppers in boiling water for 3 minutes and drain well. Chop the reserved tops.

Heat the oil in a pan and fry the onion until transparent. Add the garlic and chopped pepper and cook for a further 5 minutes, then mix in the rice, pineapple, oregano, miso and seasoning. Stir well.

Spoon the filling into the peppers, sprinkle over the breadcrumbs and place in an ovenproof dish. Cover with foil and bake in a moderate oven, 350°F, Gas Mark 4 for 30–40 minutes.
Serves 4

Black Bean and Vegetable Casserole

12 oz. (scant 2 cups) black beans,
  soaked overnight and drained
sea salt
2 tablespoons vegetable oil
2 large onions, sliced
4 sticks celery, sliced
4 carrots, sliced

2 parsnips, sliced
1 clove garlic, crushed
1 tablespoon tomato purée
1 teaspoon miso
freshly ground black pepper
chopped fresh parsley to garnish

Put the beans into a pan with fresh cold water and bring to the boil. Cover and simmer for 2 hours, adding salt towards the end of cooking. Drain and reserve the liquid.

Heat the oil in a flameproof casserole and fry the onions gently for 5 minutes. Add the vegetables and garlic and continue to fry for a further 5 minutes. Stir in the drained beans, tomato purée, miso, ¾ pint (2 cups) of the reserved bean liquid and seasoning to taste.

Cover and cook in a moderate oven, 350°F, Gas Mark 4 for 1 hour. Adjust the seasoning and serve garnished with the parsley.
Serves 4

FISH, MEAT AND POULTRY

Stuffed Mackerel Baked in Yogurt

4 mackerel, or other oily fish
2 tablespoons oil
1 onion, finely chopped
1 red pepper, seeded and chopped
4 oz. (2 cups) fresh wholemeal
  (wholewheat) breadcrumbs
1 tablespoon chopped fresh parsley
2 oz. (½ cup) walnuts, chopped
beaten egg

sea salt
freshly ground black pepper
¼ pint (⅔ cup) natural
  (unflavored) yogurt
4 tablespoons double (heavy) cream
Garnish:
sprigs of fresh parsley
lemon wedges

Wash the mackerel, remove the heads and fins, slit along the underside and gut (clean) the fish.

Heat the oil and fry the onion and pepper for 3-4 minutes. Add the breadcrumbs, parsley, walnuts, a little beaten egg to bind the mixture and seasoning. Mix well. Fill the mackerel with the stuffing and place in a greased ovenproof dish.

Mix the yogurt and cream together, add seasoning to taste and pour over the fish. Bake in a moderate oven, 350°F, Gas Mark 4 for 25 minutes.

Serve garnished with the parsley sprigs and lemon wedges.
Serves 4

Risotto with Shellfish

1 ½ pints (3 ¾ cups) water
1 glass white wine
1 bouquet garni
2 pints (2 ½ pints) mussels, cleaned
4 tablespoons oil
1 onion, chopped
8 oz. (1 cup + 2 T) brown rice
1 clove garlic, crushed

1 red pepper, seeded and chopped
2 large tomatoes, skinned and
  chopped
8 oz. (1 ⅓ cups) peeled prawns
  (shelled shrimp)
sea salt
freshly ground black pepper

Put the water, wine and bouquet garni into a pan and bring to the boil. Add the mussels and cook for 4-5 minutes, or until they are open. Discard any which do not open. Strain and reserve the stock. Shell the mussels, leaving a few unshelled for garnishing.

Heat 2 tablespoons of the oil in a pan and fry the onion for a few minutes until soft. Add the rice and garlic and fry for a further 2 minutes, stirring to prevent the rice from sticking. Add 1 pint (2 ½ cups) of the reserved stock, bring to the boil and simmer gently for 45 minutes, adding more stock if necessary.

Heat the remaining oil in a pan and fry the pepper for 5 minutes, then add the tomatoes, prawns (shrimp) and mussels. When the rice is cooked, add the shellfish mixture and seasoning and mix carefully with a fork.

Garnish with the reserved mussels and serve with grated cheese handed separately.

Serves 4

MUSHROOM AND NUT PILAFF *(page 44)*
(Photograph: Mushroom Growers' Association)

Herrings in Oatmeal

4 herrings, or other oily fish
sea salt
freshly ground black pepper
squeeze of lemon juice

oil for shallow frying
4 oz. (⅔ cup) oatmeal
sprigs of fresh parsley to garnish

Wash the herrings and remove the heads, tails and fins. Slit along the underside and gut (clean) the fish. Open out each fish, place the cut side down on a board and press firmly on the backbone to flatten the fish. Turn the fish over and remove the backbone, then sprinkle with salt, pepper and a squeeze of lemon juice.

Coat the fish in the oatmeal, pressing it on well with a palette knife. Fry in hot shallow oil for 4–5 minutes on each side and drain on kitchen paper.

Serve hot, garnished with parsley sprigs.

Serves 4

Stuffed Cabbage

12 medium cabbage leaves
sea salt
1 tablespoon oil
1 onion, finely chopped
1 clove garlic, crushed
2 oz. (½ cup) mushrooms, sliced
1 oz. (¼ cup) walnuts, chopped
6 oz. (1 cup) cooked brown rice

8 oz. (1 cup) cooked chicken,
    chopped
1 tablespoon tomato purée
1 teaspoon miso
½ tablespoon chopped fresh parsley
½ tablespoon chopped fresh thyme
8 fl. oz. (1 cup) stock

Blanch the cabbage leaves for 2 minutes in boiling, salted water, then plunge into cold water. Drain well and remove any coarse stem.

Heat the oil in a pan, add the onion and garlic and fry over a gentle heat until soft. Stir in the mushrooms and nuts, and fry for 5 minutes, then add the rice, chicken, tomato purée, miso, herbs and salt to taste. Remove from the heat.

Put a spoonful of the stuffing on each cabbage leaf and fold to make a square parcel. Place in an oiled ovenproof dish and pour over the stock. Cover with a lid or foil and bake in a moderate oven, 350°F, Gas Mark 4 for about 30 minutes. Serve with a tomato sauce.

Serves 6

Pinto Bean and Chicken Hot Pot

8 oz. (1¼ cups) pinto beans,
  soaked overnight and drained
sea salt
2 tablespoons olive oil
1 onion, sliced
2 cloves garlic, crushed
8 oz. piece of gammon (ham), cut
  into cubes
1 red pepper, seeded and shredded

1¼ pints (3 cups) stock
4 tomatoes, skinned and chopped
1 teaspoon dried oregano
½ teaspoon ground saffron
8 oz. (1 cup) cooked chicken, cut
  into large dice
freshly ground black pepper
chopped fresh parsley to garnish

Cover the beans with water, bring to the boil and simmer for 1½ hours, until tender, adding salt towards the end of cooking.

Heat the oil in a flameproof casserole and fry the onion until soft. Add the garlic, gammon (ham) and red pepper and continue cooking for a further 5 minutes. Gradually add the stock, bring to the boil and add the drained beans, tomatoes, oregano, saffron, chicken and seasoning.

Cover and cook in a moderate oven, 350°F, Gas Mark 4 for 1 hour. Serve sprinkled with the parsley.
Serves 4

Oat Flan

4 oz. (1 cup) plain (all-purpose)
 flour
sea salt
4 oz. (½ cup) margarine
4 oz. (1 generous cup) rolled oats
water to bind

Filling:
2 tablespoons oil
1 large onion, sliced
2 eggs
¼ pint (⅔ cup) milk
4 oz. (1 cup) Cheddar cheese,
 grated
2 oz. (¼ cup) cooked ham, diced
sea salt
freshly ground black pepper
4 mushrooms, sliced

Sift the flour and salt into a bowl and rub in the margarine. Mix in the oats and add sufficient water to make a stiff dough. Turn onto a floured surface, roll out and press into an 8 inch flan ring (pie pan) and chill.

Heat the oil in a pan and fry the onion gently until transparent. Mix the eggs and milk together, then add the cheese, ham, seasoning and the cooked onion.

Pour the mixture into the flan case (pie shell), arrange the sliced mushrooms around the edge and bake in a moderately hot oven, 375°F, Gas Mark 5 for 35–40 minutes.
Serves 4

OAT FLAN
(Photograph: RHM Foods Limited)

Cassoulet

1 1/2 lb. (3 1/2 cups) haricot (navy)
  beans, soaked overnight and
  drained
sea salt
3 tablespoons oil
2 onions, sliced
1 lb. belly of pork (fatty pork), cut
  into cubes
1 lb. mutton, cut into cubes

1 lb. smoked gammon (ham), cut
  into cubes
6 tomatoes, skinned and chopped
1 1/2 pints (3 3/4 cups) stock
1 bouquet garni
2 cloves garlic, crushed
freshly ground black pepper
2 oz. (1 cup) fresh wholemeal
  (wholewheat) breadcrumbs

Cover the beans with cold water, bring to the boil and simmer for
1 1/2-2 hours, adding salt towards the end of cooking.

   Heat the oil in a large pan, add the onions, pork, mutton and
gammon (ham) and fry briskly for 5 minutes. Stir in the tomatoes,
stock, bouquet garni, garlic and seasoning and simmer for 20
minutes.

   Place the drained beans and the meat mixture in alternate layers in
a deep casserole. Sprinkle with the breadcrumbs and cook,
uncovered, in a moderate oven, 325°F, Gas Mark 3 for 2-3 hours.
Remove the bouquet garni.
Serves 8-10

Bacon-stuffed Potatoes

4 large potatoes
2 oz. (1/4 cup) butter
3 oz. (5 slices) bacon, rinded,
  chopped and fried
a little milk

1 oz. (1/4 cup) walnuts, chopped
2 oz. (1/2 cup) cheese, grated
1 tablespoon chopped fresh parsley
sea salt
freshly ground black pepper

Scrub the potatoes well, prick with a fork and bake in a moderately
hot oven, 400°F, Gas Mark 6 for 1-1 1/2 hours.

   When cooked, cut off the tops of the potatoes lengthwise and
scoop out the centres, taking care to keep the skins intact. Mash the
potato in a bowl, and add the butter, bacon, milk, nuts, cheese,
parsley and seasoning.

   Fill the potato shells with the mixture and bake in a moderately
hot oven, 375°F, Gas Mark 5 for 15 minutes.
Serves 4

Peasant Stew

12 oz. (1⅔ cups) chick peas
  (garbanzos), soaked overnight and
  drained
sea salt
2 tablespoons olive oil
2 large onions, sliced
4 rashers (slices) streaky bacon,
  chopped
1 clove garlic, crushed
1 lb. belly of pork (fatty pork), cut
  into cubes

1 × 14 oz. can tomatoes
2 large carrots, sliced
2 potatoes, diced
2 sticks celery, chopped
1 bay leaf
1 teaspoon chopped fresh thyme
1 teaspoon chopped fresh parsley
freshly ground black pepper

Put the chick peas (garbanzos) into a pan and cover with cold water. Bring to the boil, cover and simmer for 1½ hours, adding salt towards the end of cooking. Drain and reserve the liquid.

Heat the oil in a pan and fry the onions, bacon and garlic gently for 5 minutes. Add the pork and cook for a further 5 minutes until browned on all sides.

Turn into a casserole with the chick peas (garbanzos) and all the remaining ingredients. Pour over 1½ pints (3¾ cups) of the reserved cooking liquid and mix well. Cover and cook in a moderate oven, 325°F, Gas Mark 3 for 2 hours. Remove the bay leaf and adjust the seasoning before serving.
Serves 4-6

Bran and Aubergine (Eggplant) Loaf

1 large aubergine (eggplant)
1 lb. (2 cups) minced (ground) beef
1 onion, finely chopped
2 tablespoons bran
1 clove garlic, crushed
½ tablespoon chopped fresh parsley
½ tablespoon chopped fresh thyme

1 tablespoon soy sauce
1 egg
sea salt
freshly ground black pepper
Garnish:
cucumber slices
radish slices

Prick the aubergine (eggplant) all over with a fork, halve, and place on a greased baking sheet. Bake in a moderately hot oven, 375°F, Gas Mark 5 for 30-40 minutes, then remove the flesh and chop finely. Mix with the remaining ingredients and spoon into a 1 lb. loaf tin, cover with foil and return to the oven for 1¼-1½ hours. Turn out and garnish with cucumber and radish slices.
Serves 4

Aubergines (Eggplant) with Bulgur Wheat

2 medium aubergines (eggplant)
3 tablespoons oil
1 onion, finely chopped
4 oz. (½ cup) minced (ground)
  cooked ham
2 oz. (⅓ cup) bulgur wheat,
  cooked
1 clove garlic, crushed

1 tablespoon chopped fresh parsley
1 teaspoon dried marjoram
2 tablespoons tomato purée
4 tablespoons (¼ cup) stock
sea salt
freshly ground black pepper
3 oz. (¾ cup) Cheddar cheese,
  grated

Slice the aubergines (eggplant) in half lengthwise, scoop out the flesh and chop finely. Heat the oil in a pan, add the onion and aubergine (eggplant) flesh and cook until softened. Add this mixture to all the remaining ingredients, except the cheese, and mix thoroughly.

Place the aubergine (eggplant) shells on a greased, ovenproof serving dish and fill with the stuffing. Sprinkle with the cheese and bake in a moderate oven, 350°F, Gas Mark 4 for 30 minutes.
Serves 4

BRAN AND AUBERGINE (EGGPLANT) LOAF
(Photograph: Carmel Produce Information Bureau)

Wholewheat Hamburgers

1 lb. (2 cups) minced (ground) beef
4 oz. (2 cups) fresh wholemeal
  (wholewheat) breadcrumbs
1 oz. (½ cup) bran
6 tablespoons milk

1 small onion, finely chopped
1 tablespoon chopped fresh parsley
sea salt
freshly ground black pepper
corn oil for frying

Combine all the ingredients together, except the oil, and mix thoroughly. With wet hands, divide the mixture into 8 equal portions and shape into thick, flat rounds.

Heat the oil in a pan and fry for 6 minutes on each side. Serve in wholemeal (wholewheat) rolls (buns) with dill pickles.
Makes 8 hamburgers

Chilli con Carne

8 oz. (¾ cup) red kidney beans,
  soaked overnight and drained
2 tablespoons corn oil
2 onions, chopped
2 cloves garlic, crushed
2 lb. (4 cups) minced (ground) beef
1 green pepper, seeded and chopped

1 tablespoon chilli powder
1 teaspoon paprika pepper
1 tablespoon wholemeal
  (wholewheat) flour
½ teaspoon sea salt
2 × 14 oz. cans tomatoes

Cook the kidney beans in boiling water for 1 hour, until almost tender, adding salt towards the end of cooking.

Heat the oil in a pan, add the onions and garlic and fry until golden. Add the meat and green pepper and fry for 5-6 minutes, stirring continuously to break up the meat. Stir in the chilli powder, paprika, flour and salt and cook for a further 2 minutes. Add the tomatoes, mix well and bring to the boil. Lower the heat, cover and simmer for 1 hour, stirring occasionally to prevent the meat from sticking. Adjust the seasoning before serving.
Serves 6

Swedish Meatballs

1 large onion, finely chopped
1 clove garlic, crushed
1 lb. (2 cups) minced (ground) beef
6 oz. (3 cups) fresh wholemeal
  (wholewheat) breadcrumbs
½ tablespoon chopped fresh thyme
½ tablespoon chopped fresh parsley
2 teaspoons soy sauce

sea salt
freshly ground black pepper
1 egg
3 tablespoons water
4 tablespoons (¼ cup) oil
½ pint (1¼ cups) tomato sauce
¼ pint (⅔ cup) natural
  (unflavored) yogurt

Mix the onion, garlic and minced (ground) beef together in a large
bowl and stir in the breadcrumbs, herbs, soy sauce and seasoning.
Whisk the egg with the water, add to the meat mixture and mix
thoroughly. With wet hands divide the mixture into 20 equal
portions and roll each into a ball.

Heat the oil in a large pan and fry the meat balls, shaking the pan
frequently, until they are golden brown. Drain on kitchen paper and
place in an ovenproof dish.

Pour the tomato sauce over the meat balls and cook in a moderate
oven, 350°F, Gas Mark 4 for 30 minutes. Ten minutes before serving
spoon the yogurt over the meat balls.
Serves 4

Aubergine (Eggplant) and Bean Casserole

8 oz. (1 cup) haricot (navy) beans,
  soaked overnight and drained
2 tablespoons oil
2 onions, sliced
4 carrots, sliced
2 sticks celery, sliced

1 lb. stewing lamb, cut into cubes
1 large aubergine (eggplant), sliced
1 pint (2½ cups) stock
sea salt
freshly ground black pepper

Cover the beans with water, bring to the boil and simmer gently for 1 hour, adding salt towards the end of the cooking time.

Heat the oil in a flameproof casserole and fry the onions, carrots and celery for 5 minutes. Remove the vegetables from the casserole and fry the lamb until browned on all sides. Return the vegetables to the casserole with the aubergine (eggplant). Pour over the stock and add the drained beans and seasoning.

Cover and cook in a moderate oven, 350°F, Gas Mark 4 for 1 hour or until the meat is tender.

Serves 4-6

AUBERGINE (EGGPLANT) AND BEAN CASSEROLE
(Photograph: Carmel Produce Information Bureau)

DESSERTS

Baked Apple with Dates

4 large cooking apples
2 oz. (6 T) dates, stoned (pitted)
  and chopped
1 oz. (3 T) raisins
1 oz. (2½ T) molasses sugar
½ teaspoon ground cinnamon
4 tablespoons water

Decoration:
4 pieces stem (preserved) ginger,
  coarsely chopped
¼ pint (⅔ cup) soured cream

Wash, dry and core the apples, and make a shallow cut through the
peel all round the centre of each. Combine the dates, raisins, sugar
and cinnamon and use this mixure to stuff the apples, pressing down
well.

   Place the stuffed apples in an ovenproof dish and pour 4
tablespoons of water around them. Bake in a moderate oven, 350°F,
Gas Mark 4 for 45 minutes, until the apples are soft.

   Fold the ginger into the soured cream and pile on top of the apples
before serving.

Serves 4

Oatmeal Syllabub

4 tablespoons medium oatmeal
3 or 4 tablespoons Scotch whisky
1 tablespoon lemon juice
2 tablespoons heather honey

¼ pint (⅔ cup) double (heavy)
  cream
twists of fresh lemon to decorate

Spread the oatmeal on a foil plate and toast for a few minutes under the grill (broiler), shaking frequently so that it browns evenly. Leave to cool.

Mix together the whisky, lemon juice and honey, then gradually whisk in the cream until the mixture stands in soft peaks. Fold in the toasted oatmeal and spoon into goblets.

Chill until required. Decorate each goblet with a twist of lemon and serve with thin sweet biscuits (cookies).
Serves 4

Nut and Apple Tart

8 oz. (2 cups) wholemeal
  (wholewheat) pastry
1 lb. (4 cups) cooking apples,
  peeled, cored and thinly sliced
2 oz. (½ cup) walnuts, chopped

2 oz. (⅓ cup) raisins
4 oz. (⅔ cup) molasses sugar
grated rind of 1 lemon (optional)
½ teaspoon ground cinnamon
milk for brushing

Divide the pastry into two equal halves. Roll out one half on a floured surface and use to line a 9 inch ovenproof plate. Mix together the apples, walnuts, raisins, sugar, lemon rind and cinnamon. Spoon this mixture onto the pastry and dampen the edge with a little cold water. Roll out the remaining pastry for the lid. Lay over the filling and trim off any overlap with a sharp knife.

Brush with the milk and make a slit in the top of the pie to allow the steam to escape. Bake in a hot oven, 425°F, Gas Mark 7 for 20 minutes, then reduce the heat to moderate, 350°F, Gas Mark 4 for a further 35 minutes.
Serves 4

Banana and Honey Flan

3 oz. (⅓ cup) butter
3 tablespoons clear honey
8 oz. (2½ cups) muesli

Filling:
4 oz. (½ cup) cream cheese
3 bananas
1 tablespoon clear honey
juice of ½ lemon
2 teaspoons (1½ teaspoons)
  gelatine
4 fl. oz. (½ cup) double (heavy)
  cream, lightly whipped

Melt the butter and honey in a pan, then add the muesli and stir well.
Place a greased 8 inch flan ring (pie pan) on a greased baking sheet,
and line with the muesli mixture, pressing well into the base
(bottom) and sides.

Bake in a moderate oven, 350°F, Gas Mark 4 for 8-10 minutes,
until golden brown. When cool, remove the flan ring (pie pan) and
place the flan case (pie shell) on a serving plate.

Beat the cream cheese until soft. Mash 2 of the bananas, then stir
into the cream cheese with the honey and lemon juice. Soak the
gelatine in 2 tablespoons of water in a heatproof bowl. Place over a
pan of gently simmering water and stir until dissolved. When cool,
mix into the banana mixture, then fold in the cream.

Turn into the prepared flan case (pie shell) and chill until set.
Decorate with the remaining banana cut into slices and dipped in
lemon juice.
Serves 4-6

Rhubarb Brown Betty

3 oz. (⅓ cup) butter
8 oz. (2½ cups) muesli
4 oz. (⅔ cup) molasses sugar
1 teaspoon ground ginger

2 tablespoons water
1½ lb. rhubarb, cut into 1 inch
  lengths

Melt the butter in a saucepan, add the muesli, sugar and ginger and
mix well. Pour the water into the bottom of a 2 pint (5 cup)
ovenproof dish, then arrange the rhubarb and muesli mixture in
layers, finishing with a layer of muesli mixture.

Bake in a moderate oven, 350°F, Gas Mark 4 for 45 minutes, until
the rhubarb is tender and the topping golden brown.
Serves 4-6

WHOLEWHEAT FRUIT PLAIT (BRAID) *(page 90)*, BANANA
AND HONEY FLAN, RHUBARB BROWN BETTY
(Photograph: Kellogs kitchen)

Brown Bread Ice Cream

3 oz. (1½ cups) fresh wholemeal
  (wholewheat) breadcrumbs
2 oz. (⅓ cup) molasses sugar
2 oz. (½ cup) hazelnuts, skinned
  and ground

4 eggs, separated
4 oz. (½ cup) castor (superfine)
  sugar
½ pint (1¼ cups) double (heavy)
  cream

Place the breadcrumbs, molasses sugar and hazelnuts on an enamel or foil plate. Toast under a hot grill (broiler) until golden brown and caramelized, stirring occasionally. (This will take about 5–8 minutes.) Leave to become quite cold.

Whisk the egg yolks in a small bowl until well mixed. In another, larger, bowl whisk the egg whites until stiff, then whisk in the sugar, a teaspoonful at a time. Beat the cream until it forms soft peaks, then fold into the meringue with the egg yolks and breadcrumb mixture. Turn into a 2½ pint (6 cup) rigid container, cover, seal and freeze.

Allow to thaw at room temperature for 5 minutes before serving in scoops.
Serves 6–8

Apricot Fool

8 oz. (1 cup) dried apricots, soaked
  overnight
½ pint (1¼ cups) natural
  (unflavored) yogurt

2 tablespoons clear honey
¼ pint (⅔ cup) double (heavy)
  cream, lightly whipped

Simmer the apricots for 20 minutes, until tender, then place in a blender with enough of the water in which they were cooked to make a thick purée. Mix the purée with the yogurt and honey. Fold the cream into the apricot mixture.

Spoon into glasses and chill before serving.
Serves 4

Prunes in Red Wine

½ pint (1¼ cups) red wine
2 tablespoons clear honey
1 teaspoon lemon juice

1 lb. (2⅔ cups) prunes, soaked
  overnight and drained
natural (unflavored) yogurt to serve

Place the wine, honey and lemon juice in a saucepan, bring to the boil and simmer for 10 minutes, then add the prunes and simmer for a further 10 minutes. Allow to cool, then chill and serve with yogurt.
Serves 6

Prune Whip

7 oz. (1¼ cups) prunes
1 tablespoon (2¼ teaspoons)
  gelatine
4 tablespoons water
¾ pint (2 cups) natural
  (unflavored) yogurt

½ teaspoon lemon juice
1 oz. (¼ cup) walnuts, chopped,
  to decorate

Cook the prunes until soft and purée in a blender with a little of the water in which they were cooked.

Soak the gelatine in the water in a heatproof bowl, then place over a pan of gently simmering water until dissolved. When cool, add to the prunes with the yogurt and lemon juice.

Spoon into glasses and leave to set. Decorate with the chopped nuts.
Serves 4

Muesli

4 oz. (1 generous cup) rolled oats
½ oz. (¼ cup) bran
1 oz. (¼ cup) grapenuts
1 oz. (3 T) sultanas (seedless white raisins)

1 oz. (3 T) raisins
1 oz. (¼ cup) nuts, chopped
1 oz. (2½ T) molasses sugar

Mix all the ingredients together thoroughly, and serve with cold milk or yogurt, to taste. Top with fresh fruit.
Serves 4

Apricot and Prune Muesli
Make as for Muesli above, but substitute 1 oz. (3T) chopped, dried apricots and 1 oz. (3T) chopped, dried prunes, for the sultanas (seedless white raisins) and raisins.

Porridge

4 oz. (1 generous cup) rolled oats
1 pint (2½ cups) water

½ teaspoon sea salt

Place the oats in a saucepan and gradually stir in the water, add the salt and bring slowly to the boil, stirring constantly to keep the porridge smooth and creamy. Simmer for 5–10 minutes until the porridge thickens.

Serve with extra salt, molasses sugar or golden (maple) syrup to taste, and single (light) cream.
Serves 4

MUESLI, PORRIDGE
(Photograph: RHM Foods Limited)

Danish Apple Charlotte

1 ½ lb. apples, peeled, cored and
  sliced
2 tablespoons clear honey
2 oz. (¼ cup) butter

4 oz. (2 cups) fresh wholemeal
  (wholewheat) breadcrumbs
1 oz. (¼ cup) wheatgerm
natural (unflavored) yogurt to serve

Cook the apples in a pan with the honey until soft. Melt the butter
and fry the breadcrumbs until golden brown, then add the
wheatgerm.

   Arrange the apples and the breadcrumb mixture in alternate layers
in a serving dish, finishing with a layer of breadcrumbs. Chill, and
serve with yogurt.
Serves 4

Hot Apricots in Brandy

2 tablespoons clear honey
4 fl. oz. (½ cup) sweet white wine
8 fl. oz. (1 cup) water
1 inch stick cinnamon
1 teaspoon lemon juice
12 oz. (1 ½ cups) dried apricots,
  soaked overnight and drained

1 tablespoon brandy
2 oz. (½ cup) flaked almonds,
  toasted
natural (unflavored) yogurt to serve

Place the honey, wine, water, cinnamon and lemon juice in a pan and
bring to the boil. Add the apricots and simmer gently for 15 minutes,
then add the brandy.

   Spoon the apricots and syrup into a serving dish, sprinkle with the
flaked almonds and serve with yogurt.
Serves 4

Date and Melon Salad

5 tablespoons clear honey
juice of 1 lemon
¼ pint (⅔ cup) water
2 Ogen melons
2 oranges, peeled and cut into
  segments

8 fresh dates, peeled, stoned (pitted)
  and quartered
1 dessert apple, peeled, cored and
  sliced
4 oz. (1 cup) black grapes, halved
  and seeded

Mix the honey with the lemon juice and water and boil for 2 minutes. Halve the melons, remove the seeds and scoop out the flesh with a ball scoop. Mix with the other fruits. Pour the cooled honey syrup over the fruit salad and divide equally between the melon shells.
Serves 4

Date Cheesecake

2 oz. (¼ cup) butter
8 oz. (2 cups) digestive biscuits
  (Graham crackers), crushed
1 egg
2 tablespoons honey
8 oz. (1 cup) curd cheese
8 oz. (1 cup) cream cheese
grated rind and juice of 1 lemon
4 fresh dates, skinned, stoned
  (pitted) and chopped

Decoration:
¼ pint (⅔ cup) double (heavy)
  cream, whipped
10 fresh dates, skinned, halved and
  stoned (pitted)
6 grapes, halved and seeded

Melt the butter in a pan, add the biscuit (cracker) crumbs and mix well. Turn into a greased 8 inch springform tin and press evenly over the base (bottom) and sides.

Mix the egg, honey, curd and cream cheeses together, then add the lemon juice and rind with the chopped dates. Turn the mixture onto the crumb case and bake in a moderate oven, 350°F, Gas Mark 4 for 30 minutes. Turn the heat off, but leave the cake in the oven for a further 30 minutes to prevent it from sinking.

When cold, remove the tin and place the cake on a serving dish. Spread a thin layer of cream on the cheesecake, then decorate with the dates, grapes and rosettes of cream.
Serves 6

Dried Fruit Salad

1 pint (2½ cups) water
2 tablespoons clear honey
1 teaspoon ground cinnamon
2 cloves
2 tablespoons lemon juice
4 oz. (½ cup) dried apricots
4 oz. (⅔ cup) dried prunes
4 oz. (2 cups) dried apples

4 oz. (½ cup) dried figs
2 oz. (⅓ cup) sultanas (seedless white raisins)
1 oz. (¼ cup) walnuts
1 oz. (¼ cup) blanched, flaked almonds
natural (unflavored) yogurt to serve

Mix the water, honey, cinnamon, cloves and lemon juice together in a pan and bring to the boil. Reduce the heat and add the apricots, prunes, dried apples and figs, cover and simmer gently for 15 minutes.

Just before serving add the sultanas (seedless white raisins) and nuts. Serve hot with yogurt.
Serves 4-6

Yogurt and Watermelon Cup

½ watermelon
½ pint (1¼ cups) natural (unflavored) yogurt
1 tablespoon dark rum

2 tablespoons clear honey
2 tablespoons wheatgerm, toasted
1 oz. (¼ cup) flaked almonds, toasted, to decorate

Scoop out the flesh of the watermelon, discarding the seeds, and cut into cubes.

Mix the yogurt, rum, honey and wheatgerm together and fold in the cubes of watermelon. Chill for one hour, spoon into glasses and sprinkle with nuts.
Serves 6

DRIED FRUIT SALAD
(Photograph: Paul Williams)

CAKES, COOKIES AND BREADS

Oat Macaroons

6 oz. (1¾ cups) rolled oats
5 oz. (¾ cup) molasses sugar
4 fl. oz. (½ cup) oil
1 egg

½ teaspoon sea salt
½ teaspoon almond essence
  (extract)

Put the oats, sugar and oil into a bowl, mix well and leave to stand for 1 hour. Add the egg, salt and almond essence (extract) and beat well.

Place teaspoonsful of the mixture onto a greased baking sheet and press flat with a wet fork. Bake in a moderate oven, 325°F, Gas Mark 3, for 15 minutes until golden brown. Leave to cool for 1 minute before removing from the baking sheet.
Makes 30

Wholewheat Gingerbread

4 oz. (1 cup) plain (all-purpose) flour
¼ teaspoon sea salt
½ teaspoon ground cinnamon
3 teaspoons ground ginger
1 teaspoon bicarbonate soda (baking soda)
4 oz. (1 cup) wholemeal (wholewheat) flour

1½ oz. (¼ cup) molasses sugar
2 oz. (⅓ cup) sultanas (seedless white raisins)
4 oz. (½ cup) butter
2 tablespoons golden (light corn) syrup
2 tablespoons molasses
1 large egg
¼ pint (⅔ cup) milk

Line a 7 × 7 × 2½ inch cake tin with greaseproof paper (non-stick parchment).

Sift the white flour, salt, spices and soda into a mixing bowl. Add the wholemeal (wholewheat) flour, sugar and sultanas (seedless white raisins). Warm the butter, syrup and molasses in a pan. Beat the egg and add the milk. Gradually mix the liquids into the dry ingredients. When well mixed, pour into the cake tin and bake in a moderate oven, 325°F, Gas Mark 3 for about 1 hour, or until just firm.

The gingerbread will improve if stored for a few days in an airtight container.

Makes one 7 inch square cake

Date Crunchies

6 oz. (¾ cup) dates, peeled, stoned (pitted) and chopped
2 tablespoons water
1 tablespoon clear honey
8 oz. (2 cups) wholemeal (wholewheat) flour

3 oz. (½ cup) molasses sugar
4 oz. (1 generous cup) rolled oats
5 oz. (½ cup + 2T) margarine, melted

Simmer the dates, water and honey in a pan until the dates are soft. Put the flour, sugar and oats in a bowl, add the margarine and mix well.

Turn half the oat mixture into a greased 7 inch square cake tin and press down. Cover with the date mixture, then sprinkle the remaining oat mixture on top and press down again. Bake in a moderate oven, 350°F, Gas Mark 4 for 55-60 minutes.

Cut into fingers (bars) while still warm, then allow to cool completely in the tin before removing carefully.

Makes 18

Bran Cookies

4 oz. (1 cup) wholemeal
  (wholewheat) flour
3 oz. (½ cup) molasses sugar
1 oz. (¼ cup) rolled oats
1 oz. (½ cup) bran
1 teaspoon bicarbonate of soda
  (baking soda)

1 teaspoon ground ginger
3 oz. (⅓ cup) unsalted (sweet)
  butter
1 tablespoon golden (light corn)
  syrup
1 tablespoon milk

Place the flour, sugar, oats and bran in a bowl, sift in the soda and ginger and mix thoroughly.

Heat the butter gently in a pan with the syrup and milk, until the butter has just melted. Pour into the flour mixture and mix thoroughly with a wooden spoon. Shape the mixture into small balls.

Set the balls well apart on a greased baking sheet. Bake in the centre of a moderate oven, 325°F, Gas Mark 3 for 15 minutes, until golden brown.
Makes 15

Rich Bran Scones (Biscuits)

7 oz. (1¾ cups) wholemeal
  (wholewheat) flour
1 teaspoon baking powder
1 oz. (½ cup) bran
½ teaspoon sea salt
2 oz. (¼ cup) margarine
1 oz. (2½ T) molasses sugar

2 tablespoons currants or sultanas
  (seedless white raisins)
1 egg, mixed with milk to make up
  to ¼ pint (⅔ cup)
milk for brushing
sesame seeds to decorate

Mix the flour, baking powder, bran and salt in a bowl and rub in the margarine. Stir in the sugar and the fruit. Beat the egg and milk together and add to the flour mixture to make a soft dough.

Turn onto a floured surface, roll out to ½ inch thickness and cut into rounds with a 2½ inch diameter cutter.

Place the scones (biscuits) on a greased baking sheet, brush the tops with milk and sprinkle with sesame seeds. Bake in a hot oven, 425°F, Gas Mark 7 for 10-12 minutes, until golden.
Makes 10

DATE AND APPLE SALAD (page 20),
DATE CHEESECAKE (page 71)
(Photograph: Carmel Produce Information Bureau)

Oat Cakes

8 oz. (2¼ cups) rolled oats
4 oz. (1 cup) wholemeal
  (wholewheat) flour
½ teaspoon sea salt

1 teaspoon baking powder
2½ oz. (5 T) lard (shortening)
cold water to mix

Mix the rolled oats, flour, salt and baking powder together in a bowl. Rub in the lard (shortening) and add enough cold water to make a firm dough.

Sprinkle some rolled oats onto a lightly floured surface, turn out the dough and knead for 2 or 3 minutes. Roll out into a round, about 7 inches in diameter and ¼ inch thick, and cut into 8 wedges.

Place on a greased baking sheet and bake in a moderate oven, 350°F, Gas Mark 4 for 25 minutes.

Serve with marmalade for breakfast, as a pleasant alternative to toast.
Makes 8

Flapjack Fingers

4 oz. (½ cup) margarine
3 oz. (½ cup) molasses sugar
1 tablespoon golden (light corn)
  syrup

1 tablespoon molasses
4 oz. (1 generous cup) rolled oats

Grease a shallow 7 inch square tin. Melt the margarine with the sugar, syrup and molasses, then stir in the rolled oats and mix thoroughly. Press the mixture evenly into the tin with a palette knife.

Bake in a moderate oven, 325°F, Gas Mark 3 for 30 minutes, until golden brown. Allow to cool slightly in the tin, then mark into fingers (bars) with a sharp knife and loosen round the edges.

When the flapjack is firm, turn it out, break into fingers (bars) and cool on a wire rack.
Makes 12

Cherry and Honey Loaf

6 oz. (¾ cup) butter
3 oz. (½ cup) molasses sugar
3 tablespoons clear honey
3 eggs, beaten
8 oz. (2 cups) wholemeal
  (wholewheat) flour

2 teaspoons baking powder
5 oz. (⅔ cup) glacé (candied)
  cherries, quartered
3 tablespoons milk

Grease and line a 2 lb. loaf tin.

Cream together the butter, sugar and honey until the mixture is light and creamy. Beat in the eggs a little at a time, continuing to beat well after each addition. Add a tablespoon of the flour with the last amount of the egg, to prevent curdling.

Sift the baking powder into the flour and add to the creamed mixture with the cherries and milk. Mix well together, then turn the mixture into the prepared loaf tin. Bake in a moderate oven, 350°F, Gas Mark 4 for 55-60 minutes. Turn the loaf out onto a wire rack to cool.

Serve sliced, with butter.

Makes one 2 lb. loaf

Old English Ale Cake

8 oz. (1⅓ cups) molasses sugar
8 oz. (1 cup) margarine
2 eggs
12 oz. (3 cups) wholemeal
  (wholewheat) flour
2 teaspoons baking powder
1 teaspoon mixed spice

¼ pint (⅔ cup) brown ale
6 oz. (1 cup) currants
6 oz. (1 cup) sultanas (seedless
  white raisins)
2 oz. (⅓ cup) raisins
3 oz. (¾ cup) walnuts, chopped
grated rind of 1 orange

Line the base (bottom) and sides of an 8 inch round cake tin.

Cream the sugar and margarine until light and fluffy, then gradually beat in the eggs with a little flour. Combine the remaining flour with the baking powder and mixed spice. Fold in approximately 3 tablespoons of the flour mixture alternately with a similar measure of brown ale. When all the flour and ale has been used, gently fold in the fruit, nuts and orange rind.

Turn the mixture into the prepared tin, and bake in a cool oven, 300°F, Gas Mark 2 for 2-2½ hours. Allow the cake to cool for 30 minutes before removing from the tin. Turn onto a wire rack to cool completely, then wrap in greaseproof (waxed) paper and store in an airtight tin for a few days before using.

Makes one 8 inch round cake

Wholewheat Chocolate Cake

4 oz. (1 cup) wholemeal
  (wholewheat) flour
2 tablespoons (unsweetened) cocoa
  powder
1½ teaspoons baking powder
4 oz. (½ cup) soft margarine
4 oz. (⅔ cup) soft (light) brown
  sugar
2 eggs

Fudge Icing:
1½ oz. (3 T) butter or margarine
3 tablespoons milk
few drops of vanilla essence
  (extract)
2 tablespoons (unsweetened) cocoa
  powder
8 oz. (1¾ cups) icing
  (confectioners') sugar, sifted
walnuts to decorate

Line two 7 inch sandwich tins (layer cake pans) with buttered greaseproof paper or non-stick parchment. Place all the cake ingredients in a large bowl, mix well, then beat for 2 minutes. Spoon into the prepared cake tins and level the surfaces. Bake in a moderate oven, 350°F, Gas Mark 4 for 35 minutes or until well risen and springy to the touch.

To prepare the icing, melt the butter with the milk over low heat. Stir in the vanilla essence (extract) and cocoa, then gradually beat in the icing (confectioners') sugar. Remove from the heat and allow to cool, beating occasionally during cooling. Sandwich the cake layers together with half of the icing then spread the remainder over the top. Decorate with walnuts.
Makes one 7 inch round cake

Parkin

½ teaspoon bicarbonate of soda
  (baking soda)
½ teaspoon sea salt
1 teaspoon ground ginger
8 oz. (2 cups) wholemeal
  (wholewheat) flour
8 oz. (2¼ cups) rolled oats

4 oz. (½ cup) butter
4 fl. oz. (½ cup) molasses
4 fl. oz. (½ cup) golden (light
  corn) syrup
2 tablespoons clear honey
2 tablespoons molasses sugar
6 fl. oz. (¾ cup) milk

Sift the soda, salt and ginger into a mixing bowl, add the flour and stir in the rolled oats. Put the butter, molasses, syrup, honey and sugar into a pan and heat gently, stirring occasionally. Remove from the heat and add the flour mixture and the milk and mix well.

Pour the batter into a greased 8 inch square cake tin. Bake in a moderate oven, 350°F, Gas Mark 4 for 50-60 minutes, or until the cake is firm to the touch. Cool in the tin for 15 minutes, then turn out onto a wire rack.

Store the parkin in an airtight tin for 1 week before eating.
Makes one 8 inch square cake

WHOLEWHEAT CHOCOLATE CAKE
(Photograph: Home Baking Bureau)

Mushroom Bread

1 oz. fresh yeast (1 cake
  compressed yeast)
¼ pint (⅔ cup) warm water
1½ lb. (6 cups) wholemeal
  (wholewheat) flour
12 oz. (3 cups) plain (all-purpose)
 flour.
1 tablespoon sea salt

1 oz. (½ cup) bran
1 teaspoon molasses sugar
1 oz. (2 T) butter
¼ pint (⅔ cup) milk
1 oz. (¼ cup) onion, finely
  chopped
8 oz. (2 cups) mushrooms, chopped

Blend the yeast with 3 tablespoons of the water. Sift the flours and salt into a warmed bowl. Add the bran and sugar and rub in the butter. Make a well in the centre and pour in the yeast liquid with the remaining water and the milk. Draw all the ingredients together and beat until the dough is smooth and comes cleanly away from the sides of the bowl.

Turn out onto a floured surface and knead for 5-8 minutes, until smooth and elastic. Place in a greased bowl, cover with a damp cloth and leave in a warm place to rise until it has doubled its bulk.

Turn out onto a floured surface and knead in the onion and mushrooms, a little at a time, using a little extra flour should the dough become sticky. Knead for 2 minutes, divide the mixture in half and shape into 2 loaves. Place in 2 greased 2 lb. loaf tins and leave in a warm place to prove until the dough rises to the top of the tins.

Bake in a hot oven, 425°F, Gas Mark 7 for 20 minutes, then reduce the heat to 375°F, Gas Mark 5 and bake for a further 30 minutes until the bread sounds hollow when tapped underneath. Cool on a wire rack.

Makes two 2 lb. loaves

Soda Bread

12 oz. (3 cups) wholemeal
  (wholewheat) flour
4 oz. (1 cup) plain (all-purpose)
  flour
1 teaspoon sea salt
1 teaspoon bicarbonate of soda
  (baking soda)

2 teaspoons baking powder
12 fl. oz. (1½ cups) buttermilk
1 egg
2 tablespoons oil

Sift the dry ingredients into a bowl. Blend the buttermilk with the egg and oil, stir into the flour mixture and mix well.

Turn the dough onto a floured surface and knead lightly until smooth. Shape into a round, flatten slightly and make two deep cuts in the dough to make a cross on the top. Place on a greased baking sheet, and bake in a moderately hot oven, 400°F, Gas Mark 6 for 35–40 minutes.

Cool on a wire rack and serve warm.
Serves 6

Granny's Quick Brown Bread

½ oz. fresh yeast (½ cake
  compressed yeast)
½ pint (1¼ cups) warm water and
  milk, mixed
1 tablespoon molasses
8 oz. (2 cups) wholemeal
  (wholewheat) flour

8 oz. (2 cups) strong white (bread)
  flour
2 teaspoons sea salt
1 oz. (2 T) butter
2 tablespoons rolled oats for
  sprinkling

Grease the base (bottom) and sides of two 1 lb. loaf tins.

Blend the yeast with 2 tablespoons of the water and milk. Dissolve the molasses in the remaining water and milk. Sift the flours and salt into a bowl and rub in the butter. Make a well in the centre and add the yeast liquid and the molasses liquid and mix to a soft dough.

Turn onto a floured surface and knead for 8 minutes until the dough is smooth and elastic. Shape the dough into two loaves and place in the prepared tins. Brush the tops with water and sprinkle with the rolled oats. Place in a greased polythene bag and leave to rise until they have doubled in size. Remove from the bags and bake in a hot oven, 450°F, Gas Mark 8 for 35–40 minutes. Turn out and cool on a wire rack.
Makes two 1 lb. loaves

Fig Loaf

4 oz. (1 1/2 cups) All Bran
4 oz. (2/3 cup) molasses sugar
4 oz. (1/2 cup) dried figs, chopped
2 teaspoons molasses

1/2 pint (1 1/4 cups) milk
4 oz. (1 cup) wholemeal
 (wholewheat) flour
2 teaspoons baking powder

Put the All Bran, sugar, figs, molasses and milk into a bowl, mix together and leave to stand for 30 minutes. Sift the flour and baking powder into the All Bran mixture and mix well.

Turn into a greased 1 lb. loaf tin and bake in a moderate oven, 350°F, Gas Mark 4 for 45–50 minutes. Turn the loaf out onto a wire rack to cool.

Serve cut into slices and spread with butter.
Makes one 1 lb. loaf

Country Bread

12 oz. (3 cups) rye flour
8 oz. (2 cups) plain (all-purpose)
 flour
1 oz. (1/2 cup) bran
1 1/2 teaspoons sea salt
2 tablespoons molasses
1/2 pint (1 1/4 cups) hot water

2 oz. (1/2 cup) wheatgerm
1/2 oz. fresh yeast (1/2 cake
 compressed yeast)
1/4 pint (2/3 cup) warm water
1 teaspoon molasses sugar
2 tablespoons oil
beaten egg to glaze

Mix together the flours, bran and salt in a bowl. Dissolve the molasses in the hot water, add the wheatgerm and stir. Blend the yeast with 3 tablespoons of the warm water. Stir the sugar into the dry ingredients and make a well in the centre. Add the yeast and cooled molasses liquid with the remaining warm water and the oil. Mix well.

Turn out onto a floured surface and knead for 5–8 minutes until smooth and elastic. Place in a greased bowl, cover with a damp cloth and leave in a warm place to rise until doubled in bulk.

Turn out onto a floured surface and knead once more for 2 minutes. Shape into a long oval loaf, place on a greased baking sheet and prove in a warm place for 30 minutes.

Brush the loaf with beaten egg and bake in a hot oven, 425°F, Gas Mark 7 for 20 minutes. Reduce the heat to 375°F, Gas Mark 5, and bake for a further 40 minutes, until the bread sounds hollow when tapped underneath.
Makes one oval loaf

FLAPJACK FINGERS *(page 78)*, FIG LOAF
(Photograph: Paul Williams)

Rye Bread

1 oz. fresh yeast (1 cake
 compressed yeast)
1 teaspoon molasses sugar
½ pint (1¼ cups) warm water
1 lb. (4 cups) rye flour
8 oz. (2 cups) strong white (bread)
 flour

1 teaspoon sea salt
½ teaspoon caraway seeds
1 tablespoon molasses
¼ pint (⅔ cup) warm milk
½ teaspoon vegetable oil
milk for brushing

Blend the yeast and sugar in half the water. Sift both the flours and the salt into a warm bowl. Add the caraway seeds and make a well in the centre of the mixture. Combine the molasses and the milk and warm slightly, then pour into the centre of the flour mixture together with the yeast liquid and the remaining water. Mix thoroughly to give a firm dough.

Turn out onto a floured surface and knead for about 5 minutes until smooth and elastic. Place in a greased bowl, cover with a damp cloth and leave in a warm place until doubled in bulk.

Turn out again onto a floured surface and knead for a further 2 minutes. Divide the dough in half and shape into 2 long loaves. Place on well-greased baking sheets and leave to rise for about 30 minutes.

Brush with milk and bake in a hot oven, 425°F, Gas Mark 7 for 20 minutes, then reduce the heat to 375°F, Gas Mark 5 for a further 20 minutes, until the loaves sound hollow when tapped underneath.
Makes two 1 lb. loaves

Nutty Bran Bread

3 oz. (¾ cup) self-raising
 (self-rising) flour
3 oz. (¾ cup) wholemeal
 (wholewheat) flour
1 oz. (½ cup) bran
½ teaspoon ground cinnamon
pinch of sea salt
1 teaspoon bicarbonate of soda
 (baking soda)

4 oz. (1 cup) nuts, chopped
1 egg
4 oz. (⅔ cup) molasses sugar
4 tablespoons oil
1 teaspoon grated lemon or orange
 rind, to taste
¼ pint (⅔ cup) natural
 (unflavored) yogurt

Grease the base (bottom) and sides of a 2 lb. loaf tin.

Mix both the flours, the bran, cinnamon, salt, soda and nuts together in a large bowl. Beat the egg with the sugar, oil, grated rind and yogurt. When well beaten, add the mixture to the dry ingredients. Mix together quickly but thoroughly.

Pour into the prepared loaf tin and bake for 1 hour in a moderately hot oven, 375°F, Gas Mark 5. Turn out onto a wire rack to cool.
Makes one 2 lb. loaf

Malt Loaf

1 lb. (4 cups) wholemeal
  (wholewheat) flour
2 teaspoons sea salt
1 oz. (2 T) butter
4 oz. (⅔ cup) currants
4 oz. (⅔ cup) sultanas (seedless
  white raisins)

2 oz. (⅓ cup) molasses sugar
1 oz. fresh yeast (1 cake
  compressed yeast)
8 fl. oz. (1 cup) warm milk
4 tablespoons malt extract

Place the flour and salt in a warm bowl and rub in the butter. Add
the dried fruit and sugar and make a well in the centre. Blend the
yeast with 3 tablespoons of the milk. Mix the malt extract with the
remaining milk and add to the dry ingredients with the yeast
mixture. Draw the ingredients together, then mix until the dough
comes cleanly away from the sides of the bowl.

Turn out onto a floured surface and knead the dough for 8
minutes, until smooth and elastic. Place in a greased bowl, cover
with a damp cloth and leave to rise in a warm place until it has
doubled in bulk.

Turn out onto a floured surface and knead again for 2 minutes,
then shape into a loaf and place in a greased 2 lb. loaf tin. Prove in a
warm place until the dough rises to the top of the tin.

Bake in a hot oven, 450°F, Gas Mark 8 for 10 minutes, then reduce
the heat to 375°F, Gas Mark 5 for 35 minutes, or until the bread
sounds hollow when tapped underneath. Turn out to cool on a wire
rack.

Makes one 2 lb. loaf

Wholewheat Bread

3 lb. (12 cups) stoneground
  wholemeal (wholewheat) flour
1 oz. (½ cup) bran
1 tablespoon sea salt
1 oz. (2 T) butter
1 oz. fresh yeast (1 cake
  compressed yeast)

1 teaspoon molasses sugar
1½ pints (3¾ cups) warm water
2 tablespoons malt extract
milk for brushing
cracked wheat for sprinkling

Mix the flour, bran and salt together in a bowl and rub in the butter. Blend the yeast with the sugar and 3 tablespoons water. Add the yeast liquid to the dry ingredients with the remaining water and the malt extract. Draw the ingredients together and beat until the mixture comes cleanly away from the sides of the bowl.

Turn out onto a floured surface and knead the dough for 8 minutes until it is smooth and elastic. Place in a greased bowl, cover with a damp cloth and leave in a warm place to rise until it has doubled in size.

Turn out onto a floured surface and knead again for 2 minutes, then cut into 4 pieces. Shape into loaves and place each loaf in a greased 1 lb. loaf tin. Cover and leave in a warm place to prove until the dough rises to the top of the tins.

Brush with milk and sprinkle with cracked wheat. Bake in a hot oven, 450°F, Gas Mark 8 for 10 minutes, then reduce the heat to 375°F, Gas Mark 5 for 30 minutes, or until the bread sounds hollow when tapped underneath. Turn out onto a wire rack to cool.
Makes four 1 lb. loaves

WHOLEWHEAT BREAD
(Photograph: Paul Williams)

Wholewheat Fruit Plait (Braid)

½ oz. fresh yeast (½ cake
  compressed yeast)
¾ pint (2 cups) warm water
1¼ lb. (5 cups) wholemeal
  (wholewheat) flour
3 oz. (1½ cups) Sultana Bran,
  crushed

1 teaspoon sea salt
1 teaspoon molasses sugar
1 oz. (2 T) butter
milk for brushing
poppy seeds for sprinkling

Blend the yeast with 2 tablespoons of the water. Mix the flour,
Sultana Bran and salt together in a bowl. Stir in the sugar and rub in
the butter. Make a well in the centre, pour in the yeast liquid and the
remaining water and mix to a firm dough.

Turn out onto a floured surface and knead the dough for 8-10
minutes until it is smooth and elastic. Place in a greased bowl, cover
with a damp cloth and leave to rise in a warm place until it has
doubled in size.

Turn out onto a floured surface and knead again for 2 minutes.
Divide the dough into 3 and shape each piece into a roll 12 inches
long. Plait (braid) the 3 rolls together, sealing the ends well. Place on
a greased baking sheet and leave to prove for 15 minutes.

Brush with a little milk, sprinkle with poppy seeds and bake in a
hot oven, 425°F, Gas Mark 7 for 25 minutes, then reduce to 375°F,
Gas Mark 5 for a further 15-20 minutes, or until the plait (braid)
sounds hollow when tapped underneath. Cool on a wire rack.

Makes one 12 inch plait (braid)

INDEX

91

INDEX